As My Mind
Unwinds

As My Mind Unwinds

31 Day Devotional/Reflectional/Confessional Ride

Jennifer Ervig

Ervig/New Harbor Press
10995 Voyager Pkwy, Ste 130
Colorado Springs, CO 80921
www.NewHarborPress.com

Ordering Information:
Quantity sales. Special discounts are available on quantity purchases by corporations, associations, and others. For details, contact the "Special Sales Department" at the address above.

As My Mind Unwinds/ Jennifer Ervig. -- 1st ed.
ISBN 978-1-63357-153-2

"The important thing is not to stop questioning. Curiosity has its own reason for existence. One cannot help but be in awe when he contemplates the mysteries of eternity, of life, of the marvelous structure of reality. It is enough if one tries merely to comprehend a little of this mystery every day. Never lose a holy curiosity."   -Albert   Einstein

Contents

I've always wanted to write a book. But excuses, valid or not, would stop me:

I'm not that good.
What would it even be about?
Everybody writes a book these days. Mine will be forever lost in a sea of published books never to be read.

However, they're exactly that; excuses. I've always been a writer. It comes naturally to me. Some say writing is becoming a lost art. They say people only want to watch videos and only two minute videos at that. Our attention spans can't handle reading anymore. Oh well...I'll carry on with this gifting I guess and let God worry about what comes of it.

When my brother died, I honestly thought that was the time to write my first book; a book on grief, as I couldn't seem to find anything to read while I was grieving that could give me what I was searching for. I believe that book is still on the horizon for me, but the timing is not now.

I'm starting with what I've already done. This is a simple compilation of different articles or blogs I've written so far at JensMindUnwinds@tumblr, during my time as a ghost blogger, and elsewhere...all in devotional format. It's a good way for me to dip my toes into the authoring a book world and simultaneously develop my coaching skills by the questions I pose throughout.

When answering the questions, please use a journal and really take some time. Pray, reflect, fight with God, scribble and repeat. I know it's annoying. Believe me! I'm the girl who always moans at the thought of taking real intentional time to dig deep and reflect, but guess what? Good coaching is a messy process that leads to beautiful results. Invest the time!

As My Mind Unwinds is exactly that. It's what I process as my mind unwinds or winds up (ha!) about the random things of life and spirituality. That's all I can tell ya about the theme of this thing. It certainly touches on a variety of things...you never know what will get my wheels turning! But I hope you'll find the purpose of this devotional to be that it helps you reflect on *anything* in life that **your** mind unwinds or winds up about and find a way to bring God into the conversation as you seek devotion to Him.

This is not your typical feel good, warm and fuzzy, 500 words or less per entry devotional. There's definitely a time and place for those but not here! This is a peek into my brain (eek) and heart (ack!) taking you on the journey of how I reconcile everything I process with who God is. Each entry is between two to four pages. It's not the usual way to bring someone along on a journey toward Christ, but I'm gonna try it. Why? Because I think it's very relational and I'm very relational. I want you to join the conversation with me as you make up your own mind in obedience to Christ.

*Side Note: I got the idea to incorporate coaching questions from Jodi Detrick's book, *The Jesus Hearted Woman*. Read it.

Let me know what you think. I can handle it. ;)

Rehab

Introductory Thoughts: What better way to start a book of devotionals than with the thought of rehab? Isn't that the reason many of us decide we need to maybe dedicate a month to daily devotionals? Because it's time for rehabilitation and recalibration? While you read this entry and contemplate the following coaching questions, I pray that God will recalibrate your efforts, remove that which damages, and your giftings will soar.

Read: Romans 12:2; Proverbs 17:22; Phillippians 4:8

Why do people enter rehab? Rehab is defined as "the action of restoring someone to health or normal life through training and therapy after imprisonment, addiction, or illness." Why would *YOU* enter rehab if you should need to?
Do you need to be restored to health and a normal life after imprisonment, addiction or illness? I know I have.

Seven years ago I had to leave "a family" of sorts that I'd been a part of for 15 years. There were some unhealthy things happening there that were poison to my soul...and the souls of others. I had no power to change it so I had to leave and it was heartbreaking.

When I left I knew I needed spiritual and emotional rehabilitation and recalibration. This is how I went about restoring my health and a normal life...if there is such a thing! Ha! Check it out:

Scripture Memorization:

I had to put goodness and truth in me to reverse the effects of what I'd experienced; and by doing this, I would be able to "test and approve what God's will is" and hopefully prevent myself from being in a similar environment for too long in the future.

READ the word every day! Memorize and "chew on" a new verse every week! It will renew your mind, strengthen your resolve and protect your heart.

A fun way to memorize scripture if you have kids is to say one together every time you enter the car. My kids and I do ours on the way to school. They have several verses memorized!

Finding a New Tribe:

I surrounded myself with new people that love and serve God like crazy! People that make me laugh and make my heart happy. These people are not perfect, but they're also not toxic. They have humble hearts, open minds, and a love for all things Jesus. I pray you let those three qualities be your standard for who gets the bulk of your time.

I Focused on What God Has for Me:

I focused on my giftings and passions. I pursued them relentlessly. I practiced singing, piano and writing to improve the arts I've been blessed with. This brought me purpose and health because doing what you're meant to do and doing it well always does.

What area of your life needs restored to health and how can you rehabilitate and recalibrate to make it happen?

Jen's Coaching Questions

1. You may not need to separate yourself from anything negative like I did to recalibrate, but what area of your life do you find needs rehab?

2. Why do you need rehab in this area?

3. What does rehab look like for you?

4. What long lasting negative impacts can we experience if we don't get the rehab we need?

5. How can delaying rehab inhibit your use of your natural and spiritual gifts?

6. What is your plan to enter rehab and recalibrate your efforts to see your gifts soar in your life for God's glory?

A Christian's Take on the Japan Quake

Introductory Thoughts: Do you all remember the earthquake in Japan in March of 2011? It was a magnitude 9.0 - 9.1 that triggered massive tsunamies. The quake resulted in 15,895 deaths, 6,156 injuries and 2,539 missing.

Nothing seems to bring out the righteous opinions of "Christians" with fingers poised to point like natural disasters. These kinds of so called Christians get my blood boiling. However, I've matured somewhat myself over the years and realize that these finger pointers aren't always made of pure evil; they're just young Christians themselves trying to figure it all out. So, please read the start of this old blog with the knowledge that I now offer more grace as grace has been offered to me.

Read: Matthew 7:5; Matthew 5:44; John 4:16; 2 Peter 3:9; Hebrews 10:30; Mark 13:32-33; 1 Thessalonians 5:17

As a Christian, it really chaps my hyde when other "Christians'" reactions to natural disasters lead people astray or simply give the rest of us real Christians a bad name. You may even be an honest Christian (meaning Christ like) but are still publicly portraying a false view of God's hand in such matters. If this is you (I know it's been me before), I pray that your church leaders and elders in the walk quickly set you straight and that you, in the future, prayerfully consider what you say before you make platform Christian statements.

Two examples of incorrect thought prompt me to blog today. First, the "GOD IS SO GOOD" YouTube video and secondly, a popular blogger's insinuation that God punished Japan for not living by the ten commandments. Let's first take a look at the error of the opinion in the YouTube video. The individual says, "Praise God for answered prayers!!! God answered us after just one day of fasting and praying! He rattled the atheists in Japan! The rest of the world better be ready! 1 day of prayer=9.0 earthquake in Japan! I can't even begin to imagine what 40 days of prayer will do!". HOW SAD! God does not grant requests to punish those we think need to be punished!

First of all, we are not to judge! In Matthew 7:5 it says , " you hypocrite! First take the plank out of your own eye, and then you will see clearly to remove the speck from your brother's eye.". This means we are to work on our own faults before we can ever begin to point out others let alone seek their punishment! God also says, "vengeance is mine" (Hebrews 10:30) and "love your enemies and pray for them" (Matthew 5:44). When he says pray, he means for their salvation not their demise! "God is love" (1 John 4:16) and "desires that none would perish but that ALL would be saved" (2 Peter 3:9). He "is not slow in keeping his promise as some understand slowness but is patient" with us giving more people a chance to be saved! (2 Peter 3:9). Therefore, we conclude that it is not okay to ask God to punish unbelievers before He is ready to judge in his own way! How dare we pray against the desire of the heart of the God we "claim" to be a child and servant of! He desires that they come to repentance! That's what we should pray for and rejoice over! Do not rejoice that sinners or atheists get hit with earthquakes and tsunamis but pray that God will use the tragedy to draw hearts near to him.

Secondly, some of you may have heard similar statements to that which the blogger I mentioned made regarding these recent events in Japan. This person was insinuating that God brought this down upon us as punishment for not abiding by the Ten Commandments. Although historically, we know that God HAS punished a sinful world before by way of a natural disaster in the story of Noah and the Ark (Genesis 6:1-9:17), I do not believe that is what's happening now. In the bible it clearly states that as the end draws near, "there will be earthquakes in various places" (Mark 13:8). This earthquake as I'm sure many other things to come, is just one of the things that has to come to pass before Jesus comes back for the redeemed. God has not all the sudden, out of the blue, decided to punish us for being evil. I believe this earthquake is part of a plan already set in place to be a SIGN for us of what is to be expected because He knows the world is an imperfect place and will already be increasingly so. Therefore this earthquake is an indication of the reality of God and that what He's said is so, such as the sign in Mark 13:8, and that His plan for salvation IS set in motion and His promises WILL be fulfilled.

So, in a way, the blogger was half right, we probably should heed the Ten Commandments but not to avoid natural disasters that God might punish us with, but to please God after we've invited Him into our hearts, to live a life full of grace that we can ONLY do by His grace, to get through the next natural disaster that WILL happen. The Ten Commandments won't save you, only the blood of Jesus will, and only the blood of Jesus can give you the power and strength to live by those commandments. AND ONLY the blood of Jesus can give you the courage to live through these natural disasters without fear as the popular hymn says " I know who holds tomorrow and I know who holds my hand."

In short, when natural disasters happen, take the the opportunity to pray for the lost... Not for their demise but for their salvation and use the opportunity as a reminder to " watch and be ready" (Mark 13:32-33) and pray continually (1Thessalonians 5:17). God bless you and watch over you. Thank you for letting me say my peace.

Jen's Coaching Questions
1. What "chaps your hyde" and gives you the feeling that Christians are giving the name Christian a bad name?
2. How have you been guilty of doing those things yourself?

3. What is the danger in making public platform Christian statements?

4. Why should we serve God out of love for Him rather than fear of what might happen to us if we don't?

Take Your Stand and Stand

Introductory Thoughts: I wrote this article as an assignment for a class. I was on fire for what I was learning at the time. I hope my passion translates through this piece and prompts you to take your stand.

Read: John 16:33; James 2:17; Ephesians 6:12

"In this world you will have trouble, but take heart! I have overcome the world!" (Jn 16:33) Wow! Discouragement and encouragement all in one sentence! Overwhelming for sure for the new Christian still finding his footing in this march called life or even the seasoned Christian who may currently be knee deep in that "trouble" mentioned above. So, we know two things: We will have trouble AND we don't have to be scared when it comes.

However, is that it? When the trouble comes do we just sit there and try not to be scared? With that faith alone? While faith that Jesus has indeed overcome the world surely does give us security and strength, I think this is a good time to point out that "faith without works is dead" or "faith without ACTION is dead or worthless." (James 2:17) What good is dead faith in keeping us from shaking in our boots? How will we take heart? We need to act out our faith and make it come alive! How do we do this in light of John 16:33? Well, let's see what the apostle Paul has to say.

We need to act out our faith and make it come alive!

First he says, "our struggle (or trouble as it's called in John) is not against flesh and blood....but against the spiritual forces of evil in the heavenly realms." (Eph 6:12) So, when our spouse is fighting with us, our children are wayward, our bodies are ill, our bank account empty, our governments unjust, our ministry efforts attacked, or when insult, depression, loneliness and discouragement consume us, even though we see these things manifested physically, the force behind it is spiritual. We're at war when we meet trouble! Whether sin or weakness on our part or someone else's causes these situations, it's committed or played out on a spiritual battlefield in the "heavenly realms".

So, that's where the trouble comes from, but how can we make our faith that Jesus has "overcome the world" alive and active? Well, we can "put on the full armor of God so that when trouble comes, we can take our stand and stand!" (paraphrase from Eph

6:11,13). We can take our position "against the devil's schemes" (Eph 6:11) and HOLD our position. Okay. What is this armor that's going to help us take our stand and stand in this spiritual battle? Well, it's not something physical we put on. Just as our battle is spiritual so is our armor. Paul tells us it's the belt of truth, breastplate of righteousness, the readiness of the gospel of peace, shield of faith, helmet of salvation and sword of the Spirit. Then, to top it all off and make it complete, prayer.

We need to put on the belt of truth. This one's important, as in most cases, it's your belt that holds the rest of your get up together. Wearing the belt of truth is done by filling ourselves with scripture and memorizing it so that the next time you think thoughts that you're not good enough or hear lies that shake your foundation (your stand) such as "you're hopeless", you'll have the truth of God's word in you that says " (you) were chosen..." (Eph 1:11) and "you... know the hope to which He has called you." (Eph 1:18).

With this, we put on the breastplate of righteousness which is living a holy life compelled by the love and example of Christ. When we have righteous living, a life defined by love, even to the extent of serving our enemies!.... in doing so, "we'll heap burning coals on (their) head(s)." (Prov 25:22) That sounds like a winning battle move to me!

We also need to have our feet fitted with the gospel of peace. Having your feet "fitted" and "ready" to march into battle if necessary. A Christian soldier must always be READY. Ready to march and to bear witness to the gospel of peace. Wherever the soldier's feet take him, he can share the gospel that can bring foundation and security to a dying or injured comrade who needs help to stand or help secure his own footing when he should start to slip and lose ground himself.

Then, there's the shield of faith "with which you can extinguish all the flaming arrows of the evil one" (Eph 6:16). Every time trouble gets thrown or shot at you, your faith will protect you, because as the popular hymn says, " you know who holds the future and you know He holds your hand."

With these, we take the helmet of salvation and the sword of the Spirit. The helmet of salvation protects us by providing assurance of salvation. Imagine your helmet has an emblem on it that when others see it they immediately recognize that you're in the Lord's army. The Spirit testifies to our salvation (Rom 8:16). When they see your helmet they're sure to notice your sword. Your sword of the Spirit is both an offensive and defensive weapon. It's offensive in that it "equips you for every good work" (2 Tim 3:14-17) and defensive in that it's a "double edged sword... judging the thoughts and attitudes of the heart." (Heb 4:12). This protects you in that you will keep check on your own thoughts and attitudes by getting into the word, as well as you can decipher who's friend or foe by the same manner.

The sword of the Spirit is both an offensive and defensive weapon

Well, there you go! A complete and shining armor to equip you to take your stand and stand, activating and giving life to your faith that He who is in you is HE who has overcome the world.

(John 4:4, 16:33). But, wait! Paul says we should add prayer (Eph 6:18).

Think of prayer as your way of communicating with your commanding officer (God) so that you may always have a way to receive guidance, battle plans, encouragement and so you can let Him know of anything you may have need of out there in the battle field. You can also pray for your fellow soldiers. And for the prayer warrior baptized in the Holy Spirit, pray in the Spirit! This is especially important in times you feel powerless, alone in the battle or feel as if all your other comrades have fallen and you're all that's left. Let Him intercede for you and remind you you're not alone. You have a comforter and a friend and a source of power in the Holy Spirit. (Acts 1:8, 2:4; Jn 14:16, 17, 26, 16:7,8)

Now, we can really take heart as John 16:33 commands! Paul's told us of the armor that will help us take our stand and stand when trouble meets us on the spiritual battlefield of life. And, through prayer, the Holy Spirit provides power and companionship. What a victorious way to enlist and really make our faith come alive! Jesus has indeed overcome the world and on that promise, by faith, you can take your stand and stand.

Jen's Coaching Questions

1. What is your favorite piece of armor as described in Ephesians? Why?

2. How can you be better at taking your stand when battles happen?

3. How would you explain to someone that the bible is a "double edged sword"?

4. How has your faith been "dead" in the past?

Baptism to Stay Afloat

Introductory Thoughts: The Holy Spirit and His power available to us can be a hard thing to grasp. Because it's hard to grasp, it can also be hard to explain. It's for this reason, that when God gives a perfect depiction through a real life scenario such as my kid's swimming lessons, I get super excited. I do realize that all who may read this book don't believe in Holy Spirit Baptism. If that's you, you have permission to pass this one over; I won't be offended...but I hope you won't. ;)

Read: Romans 8; Acts 1:8, Acts 2

"Ugh! I've done it again! I'm such a failure! I am too weak and therefore will never be effective for God or any call He places on my life....."

If we're all honest, we've all proclaimed something similar to ourselves whether audibly or thoughtfully in a moment of unintentional or unexpected sin. We love the Lord. We've confessed our sins and asked Him into our hearts and we take up our cross daily....only to stumble and drop it too many times to count, but more than enough times to make us feel like powerless failures.

We know that Paul himself admitted that he finds himself doing the things he doesn't want to do and not doing the things he wants to or knows he should do (Rom 7:15, NIV). Often in despair and anguish over failing again in our own human strength, we find ourselves singing the lyrics of a popular christian song, "Do you still feel the nails every time I fail? Can you hear the crowd cry crucify again?....." We are devastated that in our human weakness, we have fallen into temptation again and we wonder, "how is it even possible to have the power or the strength to stand firm for Jesus?

Remember Peter? Remember the devastation and heartbreak he experienced when he heard the rooster crow (Luke 22:54-62, NIV)? He had a powerful love and dedication to Jesus and thought himself firm and strong enough that it seemed incredulous to him that he could ever possibly deny Jesus and let him down in that way. However, the truth emerged and Peter realized that no matter how much you love Jesus and no matter how strong you are, you are still weak in your own power.

God knows this of us and that is why He provided an answer to our frailty. God knows we fail, but if our hearts are truly repentant, He has prepared a gift especially for us...to help us in our weakness.

This gift is the baptism in the Holy Spirit. He is part of the God Head three in one(Mark 1:9-11, NIV) and gives us power to do the things God asks of us (Romans 8:26 and Acts 1:8, NIV).

We see evidence of the benefits of receiving the baptism in the Holy Spirit as our counselor, again in Peter. On the day of Pentecost, (Acts 2, NIV) just weeks after Peter so miserably failed Jesus by denying him because he was afraid of the reactions of the people, we find him BOLDY addressing the curiosity of the crowds to the happenings of Pentecost by preaching his first sermon recorded in Acts, subsequently causing 3000 to be saved ! The same man who was cowardly only weeks before has now made a powerful friend in the Holy Spirit who gives him boldness and strength to do the things he ought to do. The Holy Spirit is available here and now to do that for you too. In that Pentecost sermon, Peter declared that " ...the promise is for you and your children and all who are far off...."(Acts 2:38-39, NIV)

Our problem in receiving the baptism in the Holy Spirit often lies in another human weakness...... the complexity of our minds and our inability to rationalize the simplicity of receiving this free and generous gift. It's like when my son, Aiden, was five years old. He was taking swimming lessons and couldn't seem to conquer the almighty back float. I'd explained to him that when swimmers are tired or weak, the ability to float is a gift God has the water provide for us to help us out. All he has to do is relax, tilt his chin up towards heaven, and open his arms wide as if

wanting a big hug from Jesus.....and then, without even realizing it or really trying, the water will mysteriously and mystically
ENABLE him and lift him up and support him! Although he was
hearing this, his five year old mind couldn't logically comprehend and trust that it's so. He'd therefore become scared and try
to do the work on his own by twisting his body and kicking his
legs which only caused him to fail and sink every time.

If we want baptism in the Holy Spirit, all we have to do is ask and
receive (Matthew 7:7-11, Acts 2:38, NIV). We don't have to force
anything. It's a free gift...the same as salvation (Romans 6:23,
NIV). It requires no work on our part but to ask and take what
God has so graciously offered us through Jesus Christ. When
the baptism is underway, the Holy Spirit will ENABLE you by
giving you His manifest presence and impressions of what to
pray. All we need to do is relax, receive and have faith to obey.

There are, however, things that can hinder us from the gift of
baptism in the Holy Spirit just as there are things that can hinder Aiden from floating. The bible shows us that obedience,
unity and time with Jesus are important in receiving this baptism (Acts 1-2, NIV) So, if you lack these, you may be hindered.
Just as Aiden needs to obey and relax as he's instructed, trust
how the water works with how he was made and spend time
practicing to float. If Aiden lacks one of these aspects, he will be
hindered from his goal of floating.

It's simple to receive the gift Jesus has for us...go to him in prayer,
ask and then, simply wait to receive. If you find you're waiting
longer than expected, check that there's nothing hindering

you from "staying afloat". But, if you're relaxed and simply tilt your chin up, and open your arms wide toward heaven to receive, you'll soon find yourself unexpectedly filled and supported by a mystical and mysterious power! Aiden's manifestation of success will be evidenced in the mysterious ability to stay afloat. Your manifestation will come with mysterious groans that words cannot express (Romans 8:26, NIV).

Jen's Coaching Questions:

1. If you're baptized in the Holy Spirit, reflect on how you received that gift. How would you explain it to someone who is yet to receive?
2. If you're not yet baptized in the Holy Spirit, what do you think the hold up may be?
3. How come no matter how much we love Jesus and no matter how strong we are, we are still weak?
4. How do you think Peter felt when he gave his first sermon on Pentecost?
5. Do you think nearly as many people would have been saved that day if Peter wasn't filled with the Holy Spirit? Why or why not?

Flushing Out that which Clogs up and Backs up

Introductory Thoughts: What we have here below is a real life TMI experience that's hilarious and also brings exceptional praise to Jesus!

Read: Acts 17:30-31, Romans 12; Matthew 22

Blech! A clogged toilet! Misery upon miseries! Especially for someone with OCD that manifests itself through germaphobia! AND as if that wasn't bad enough, it was MY fault. AND if THAT wasn't bad enough, it was happening at work! Some of you are probably completely grossed out by now, but I know

most of you are intrigued by the drama of such an everyday ca-
lamity that we all relate to! What's more....that I'm WILLING
to write about it! Let me tell you, I wasn't really "willing" to
write about this except that God used this dreadful experience
to "flush out" some refuse clogging up my own life, and He performed one of those rare actual miracles that bears witnessing
to! I cannot deny my Lord the opportunity to be praised for His
grace and love toward little ole me and my "every day calami-
ties." The fact that such a miracle comes by way of a dirty toilet of my doing, well....that must be another answer to my daily
prayer of "Lord, make me humble." So now that I've tickled your
ears and wrinkled your noses, let's get to the ordeal.

The typical weekday at work on my job as a nanny in a posh
neighborhood in Mukilteo for an incredibly gorgeous and sweet
little 23 month old girl was not going so well. Certainly not because my job isn't the best job in the world, because it is! But because of my attitude. Oh, the rotten attitude...the demise of all
things lovely. How can I be depressed and upset when I work in
a nearly one million dollar home overlooking the Puget Sound?
What a blessing, right? I get to take care of a lovely little girl in
a dream land location, and I even get to bring my kids with me!
This is the dream job of all moms! Especially when it's always
been my dream to live on the water in a well kept neighborhood
with friendly people...If I can't live here, I at least get to work
here and enjoy it three days a week!

A rotten attitude... the demise of all things lovely.

Well, that's just it. As much as I do love and cherish my job and relish the location, it also makes me melancholy, longing for the home to be mine! I wish I could live there every day and start feeling sorry for myself and the humble $165,000 home I actually live in, in a not-so-well-kept neighborhood. I become ungrateful and forget the many blessings I do have and begin to wallow in my sorrow.

As this series of bad attitudes was beginning to over take me, I went on with my day. Everything seemed to be going wrong due to my "woe is me" attitude and I began to feel upset to my stomach...You all know what happened next..."UGH!" I thought! I hate, as my grandma calls it, "doing my chores" at work or any public place for that matter! Then, the unthinkable...it didn't flush! "Oh no! Can my day get any worse?" Remember, I have germaphobia, so plunging toilets is not my thing. I tried every-thing. I poured hot water in the bowl and also dish soap. I went through cycles of letting it sit and re-flushing every 15 minutes. It always filled back up! Every stinkin' time (pun intended)! I prayed, "God, PLEASE don't let my boss come home before this gets taken care of."

So of course, she came home early.

I was mortified! "No! No! No! I can't get this unclogged and they'll use the toilet tonight and know it was me! How embar-rassing! Plus, they'll think me rude for not 'taking care of it!'" My boss came home, but quickly went upstairs to her home office. "Whew... I still have a chance." I continued my 15 minute un-clogging cycles. In between each one, I got more depressed and even began to get teary eyed. This was as the famous Alexander would say, "a terrible, horrible, no good, very bad day."

In between one of these cycles, I logged on to FaceBook to divert my mind. As I scroll through my news feed, I came across a post by my pastor that read, "When we want God and a bunch of other stuff, then that means we have thorns in our soil" (#CrazyLove by Francis Chan). Wow! THAT struck a chord of conviction in me!

I want God. I surely and truly do, but I keep letting desire for "this other stuff" to swell up in me too. It causes a giant clog of refuse that backs up my spiritual life! God wants me to want ONLY Him! The Bible says, "...He commands everyone to put away idols and worship only Him..." (Acts 17:30-31). Wanting things as much as or more than God makes them idols in my life. The Bible also says, "Don't copy the behavior and customs of this world, but be a new and different person with a fresh newness in all you do and think. Then you will learn from your own experience how his ways will really satisfy you" (Romans 12:2).

This conviction was promptly followed by me getting down on my knees and asking for forgiveness! I prayed, "Lord, forgive me for placing such high priority on these desires and allowing it to steal my joy in you." I then added in complete desperation, "Could you PLEASE unclog this toilet for me?"

I waited a moment in His presence and heard His answer in my spirit, "Go flush the toilet."

"Okay," I said. I went and did it. NOTHING happened. It filled right back up again! "Aargh! I sincerely thought I heard God tell me to flush the toilet." I stamped back to the living room. "I must be really off in my spiritual walk, because I can't even hear right from the Lord anymore!"

I was so frustrated and let down! God immediately spoke to me in my spirit again, "For goodness sake, CALM DOWN, Jennifer! Relax. I told you what to do. Now, just trust and obey. Do you not think I know what you're concerned and worried about and what's important to you?"

I went to peruse FaceBook again. The instant I calmed down and took my mind off it, I heard from the other end of the house the most joyous sound! FLLLLUUUUUSHH!...gurgle, gurgle, whooosh! "Woohoo! Thank you, Jesus!" The toilet just miraculously unclogged itself when I was no where near it! "Thank you, Jesus!"

An intense feeling of relief washed over me, along with overwhelming love and amazement that the Almighty God not only cares about me, my life and my eternity, but even about my clogged toilet! I knew exactly what had just happened. God performed a tiny miracle to show His love for me and unclogged my back up, both spiritually and within the porcelain throne. I praised him for several minutes, and then realized the message was two fold. If God cares about my toilet, He also knows my desires for a nice home, along with all my other dreams. This doesn't mean God is going to give me these things, but it does mean He sees me, hears me, and knows me. All He asks is the same in return (Matthew 22:37).

Jen's Coaching Questions

1. What miracle has God done for you lately?
2. How are you sharing the experience of your miracle with others?
3. How do you know God sees you, hears you and knows you?
4. What is clogging you and backing you up?

Rocks and Fallen Logs

Introductory Thoughts: No, Rocks and Fallen Logs is not another poop story! :) The opening poem and inspiration of this blog is something I memorized growing up. Why? Because it was always framed hanging in the bathroom (ha...so I guess this post does relate to the bathroom after all!) Anyway, I always thought it was beautiful and it finally dawned on me what it really meant.

Read: Acts 20:24

I removed rocks and fallen logs
from our little stream
and the brook lost it's laughter
forgot it's song.
Then, I understood why when I prayed,
"Oh, Lord, take all my troubles away,"
The answer came,
"Are you sure you want this, my child?" -author unknown

Rocks and fallen logs. Things we see as blemishes, hindrances, failures, battle wounds or scars. We're ugly, there's things in our way of what we think we want, failures and storms have left their trail of debris, battles and traumas have left their marks.... their scars. So, we feel the need to TAKE CONTROL and fix it.... or we ask God to. We remove them. Obsessing about make-up, clothes, and plastic surgery, denying failures and refusing to own up to them. We avoid obstacles and take the easy road and we bury trauma and pain deep down not dealing with it head on.

 But, in all that struggle to "remain beautiful" by our own standards, or what we think the world's standards are, by avoiding obstacles and risks, we lose ourselves! We lose our joy, our joy in the LORD! We forget our song! Without our joy, there's nothing to bring life to our beauty. There's no music to inspire the lyrics! Without our song,...... we have no identity, no voice.

 There is nothing in this world that will show your true character more than when you're in the middle of a trial. When you're using all you have and all you are to conquer a problem, deal with grief, rise to a challenge, then that's when you in your simplest and purest form shines. That's when you find out who you really are, and what makes you beautiful. When you're in the middle of something that takes all you've got to get through it or over it, your true self emerges and there's nothing you can do to hide it, because you're so engrossed in the task at hand, that all you can be is yourself and it's impossible to care about anything else. Run the race! Roll right over it like beautiful bubbling, laughing streams of water! Forget yourself and your ideals of perfection. Let your song, your testimony, be heard. Know that it makes you all the more beautiful. "24 However, I consider my life worth nothing to me; my only aim is to finish the race and complete the task the Lord Jesus has given me—the task of testifying to the good news of God's grace." (Acts 20:24)

Jen's Coaching Questions:
1. Describe a time when you've "lost your laughter and forgotten your song". Why did that happen?
2. Why are troubles good for us?
3. Why do trials make us more beautiful?

Ding Dong Bin Laden's Dead? Well, Yes and No

Introductory Thoughts: Let's face it. Our favorite part of the movie or the story is when the bad guy goes down! The Wicked Witch of the West, Captain Hook, Voldemort, etc... But those are stories. And, when we are in real life, we need to remember we're dealing with genuine people that GOD Himself created in His image. So, how do we reconcile our joy of good over evil (like when Bin Laden died in 2011) with the reality that people are involved and somebody indeed is going down without hope?

Read: They're down below YO!

As a christian, this Bin Laden thing leaves me with a mix of emotions. Let's look at the following scriptures:

Ezekiel 18:23 Do I take any pleasure in the death of the wicked? declares the Sovereign Lord. Rather, am I not pleased when they turn from their ways and live?

Proverbs 24:17 "Do not rejoice when your enemy falls, and do not let your heart be glad when he stumbles".

2 Peter 3:9 The Lord is not slack concerning His promise, as some men count slackness; but is longsuffering to us-ward, not willing that any should perish, but that all should come to repentance"

Those scriptures show us over and over again, that we should be sad when one is lost forever to burn in eternity, whether friend or foe. God loves all humans and wishes them all to choose Christ and I believe mourns when one doesn't. **HOWEVER**, clearly, Osama Bin Laden did not choose Christ. He made his own bed and now has to lie in it. Thank God for our troops who are not only fighting for us but the whole world. They worked hard to do what they HAD TO DO, and got the job done! May they be blessed and shown every kind of affection and appreciation. As a country, and as a Christian, feel free to rejoice in the triumph of good over evil. I was reminded by a friend today that the children of Israel have a song that is sung even now over the death of Pharaoh and thousands of his troops. It is okay to rejoice in good over evil for our God is a just God and demands justice. We see this in the following verses:

Proverbs 21:15 "When justice is done, it brings joy to the righteous but terror to evildoers."

Proverbs 11:7 "When a wicked man dies, his hope perishes; all he expected from his power comes to nothing."

Proverbs 16:5 "The LORD detests all the proud of heart. Be sure of this: They will not go unpunished."

So, there you go. The "proper" response for a Christian to something like this? Well, every situation is different. But, if *I'm* taking and handling scripture correctly, AND knowing the heart of my Savior, my response is this.... to have immense joy over the victory of our troops and the realization of justice, but to continue to pray for the salvation of my enemies....that none should perish.

Jen's Coaching Questions
1. Do you find yourself mourning or rejoicing when a bad man dies?
2. How often do you pray for your enemies?
3. Do you agree with Proverbs 24:17? Why or why not?
4. Who is someone you could be praying for so that they come to repentance and don't perish?

Add Your Flavor; Shine Your Light

Introductory Thoughts: Satan likes to tell us we're a distraction or we're conceited or we're sub par, but we've always got something to offer and a reason to offer it.

Read: I Corinthians 12:12-27; Matthew 5:16; Ephesians 2:10; Proverbs 22:29; I Peter 4:10

What are you good at? What do you enjoy doing? Does the world know? Recently, I realized I'd been talking myself out of doing things because whether I like it or not, whether I have an ounce of talent or not, I shouldn't put those things out for display because there's so many others that shine more and I need to step back and let them shine.

But what if my light just added to theirs? What if my spin on what someone else is already saying and doing isn't white noise but just makes their message richer?

There is NOTHING new under the sun. It's true. However, people are always seeing the same old thing with new eyes and sharing it with clearer truth.

An apple will always be an apple; but when an artist paints it, when a chef carves it into a rose or bakes it into a pie, when a writer uses its properties as an illustration to make a point about life, that apple that's simply been an apple since the beginning of time takes on new importance and meaning for different people over and over and over again.

I love to write
I love to teach
I love to sing
I love to decorate homes and parties
I love to paint

I have varying amounts of talent in each of these areas, and there is ALWAYS someone better than me, but just like when I was in a choir, my alto or soprano voice may only occasionally be the star of the show, but the rest of the time it's adding my own flavor to make the rest of the choir fuller, more beautiful. Without my voice, you might not hear the rest of the talented vocalists the same way... and that could be a shame.
5.

Please make your gifts known. I want us all to add our touch to the world. We're better together and I don't wanna be cheated out of the perfect experience.

Jen's Coaching Questions
1. What is it that you love to do?
2. Why do you love doing those things?
3. What does it look like to constantly ask yourself how you can better do what you're already doing?
4. How can you do those things to serve others?
5. If you knew someone was not using their gift around you because they thought YOU were better at it, what would you say to them?
6. What are your thoughts on this statement: "If there's someone better at what I'm doing, I'm off the hook and don't have to share my giftings."

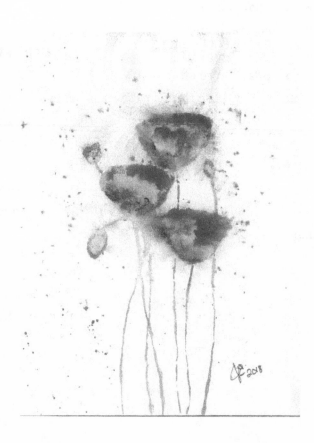

Find Your Lane and Stay in it

Introductory Thoughts: Nothing can be more frustrating than driving in the wrong lane. Maybe you're in the lane where everyone is going slow, maybe you're in a far lane that makes it near impossible to get to the one you want to be in in time. It's important to find our lane and then stay there whenever possible. Being in the right lane gets us where we're going in the most efficient way.

Read: Colossians 3:17; Romans 12; I Corinthians 12

"Find your lane and stay in it!" I first heard this piece of wisdom from Danice Squires at a women's event at my church. Since then, I often find myself meditating on it and its implications. What she's saying is find out what you're good at and stick to it!

When we discover our giftings, our God given talents and abilities, develop them, and put them to work, **only then**, are we truly happy AND truly being used as God intended.

Here's another little tidbit to chew on, " if we try to be good at everything, we won't be great at anything." I don't know about you, but I don't just want to be okay at something, I want to excel! I want to flourish at what I'm naturally good at and happy doing! Now, that's not to say that there won't always be someone out there that's better than me, cause there will be. I may be a singer, writer, speaker, a social butterfly, BUT there will always be someone with a better voice, someone wittier with their words, more eloquent of speech, and more charismatic and fun to be around.

All I know is I don't wanna waste my time. Colossians 3:17 says, "whatever you do, whether in word or in DEED, do it in the name of the Lord Jesus, giving thanks to God the Father through Him." That means everything we do, we should do as a representative of Christ! Which means, we better be doing our ABSOLUTE BEST! No excuses! I'm not wasting my time by spreading myself out too thin, trying to give time and energy to be good at as many things as I can. That won't serve the purpose of Colossians 3:17 in complete obedience. I need to find my one, or few things, that are God ordained talents and abilities and really focus on them!

By doing this, I'll also save myself a lot of stress and disappointment. I have seen the people who want to be "singers" try to sing to EVERYONE's dismay, when all the while they could be putting on AMAZING puppet shows for children's ministry or whatever the case may be! I've also seen people who wish they could write, start a blog when they could be spending their time developing their music ministry!

Clues you may be in the wrong lane? Nobody compliments you or pats you on the back after you sing, write, cook, decorate etc, no one ever recommends you to do those jobs when the opportunity arises, and you feel self conscious and doubt your ability after having done said deeds. Clues you're in the right lane? The opposite of all the aforementioned happens AND your efforts produce fruit for the Kingdom of Heaven!

So, find your lane and stay in it! Find out what makes you groove, God groove, and causes those around you to groove when you're grooving! Ha ha! Then, all will be truly groovy.

Jen's Coaching Questions
1. Explain why you believe you either are or are not in the right lane?
2. We've often heard " you can be anything you want to be and do anything you set your mind to". Do you agree or disagree and why?
3. How are your efforts producing fruit?
4. If you need to make a lane change, how do you plan on doing it?

Might You Have a Mite?

Introductory Thoughts: Looking back on this post, I now realize I sounded a little self righteous; pray for me for that. However, I still believe in my point. I'd be interested to hear your perspectives. Please drop me a line at jensmindunwinds@ tumblr if you should so desire.

This is also a good follow up post to Find Your Lane and Stay in It.

Read: James 3:1; Luke 21:1-4; I Peter 4:10; Romans 8:28

Sometimes I'm surprised by people's use of scripture. It's interesting how a passage of scripture can be "used" to defend many varying....VARYing.....down right opposite, twisted and far fetched points of view and personal agendas. As teachers, preachers, writers, bloggers and simple everyday christian witnesses, we best better be careful that we're using the word of God correctly. We WILL BE held accountable! (James 3:1) Look it up! :)

Today, I came across a blog commenter's interesting use of scripture in response to me to support the view of a blog I was reading and disagreeing with. The blog said this, " I want a church with bad sound...and painfully amateur 'special music' now and then." The point was to say that the church should allow anyone and everyone to offer whatever "gift" they have that they WANT to give even if they're not good at it because as Christians, we should let everyone express themselves and not criticize. Sorry, but I disagree. I believe, rather, we should support everyone in finding their true talent and then give them every opportunity to display THAT gifting...the one God meant for them to have. In this way, God gets to showcase His splendeur through us the way HE originally intended. In this way, both receiving and giving ends of the "gift" can be at peace and full of joy from the experience, GIVING GOD ALL THE GLORY. :)

The aforementioned commenter disagreed with me and their scriptural support was the use of the story of the widow's mite found in Luke 21:1-4. You know the story. The widow wanted to give to Jesus, so she put in her very last mite....all she had to live on... into the offering, from a pure heart of only wanting to serve and give what she can. I can see his point, and the point of the blogger.... we definitely SHOULD give people EVERY opportunity to give all that they have if that's their heart's desire.

We should NEVER keep anyone from serving Jesus and giving if they have something to give. WAIT. Back up. Did you catch that? I said, "...if IF IF they HAVE HAVE HAVE something to give". They missed a little something in their choice of supporting scripture. The widow HAD something to give. It may have only been a mite, but she HAD it, she owned it.... therefore, she could give it AND should rightfully experience the joy of sharing! THAT is honorable.

It's the people who "think" they have "a certain" something to give and are trying to give it that I don't agree with. We are not meant to have the same gifts. Sometimes some of us wish we were singers, dancers, poets, artists, etc. but we're simply not. Fact is though, we all do have something to give. God has given us ALL gifts! and just like the widow, WE SHOULD use them to serve others! We're commanded to! (1 Peter 4:10) Look it up! :)

Anyway, in short, honor God and His kingdom by developing all that HE created you to be. Not what you wish you could create yourself to be! Also, when choosing scripture, make sure it remotely relates to what you're trying to prove. All things work together for good for those who are called according to HIS PURPOSE (Romans 8:28) wink wink...HIS purpose. With your talent/gifts and your preaching, put forth HIS PURPOSE and it'll be AALLLLL GOOOOD!

Jen's Coaching Questions

1. Why or why not would you find yourself agreeing with me or the blogger and commenter?
2. If you tried to offer something that's not yours, how would you feel?
3. Again, if you tried to offer something that's not yours, how would your gift be perceived?
4. How would you feel if you found out someone gave you something that wasn't theirs to give?

I Don't Like You I Love You

Introductory Thoughts: Fair warning; due to my abrupt style, this one holds the potential to offend, but please know my heart as you read.

Read: Luke 9:23; 1 Peter 4:8

I don't like christians. I don't like people. I don't like God. I don't like christians because all too often they give Jesus a bad name. I don't like people because they're not Christ-like and I don't like God because I'm obsessed with myself.

As a self proclaimed Christ follower who practices pentecostal faith, I won't typically call myself a Christian. The term Christian used to mean "christ-like" but does it anymore? I think not. The dictionary may say so, but I think when most people hear "christian" it's synonymous with self-righteous jerk, gay basher, intolerant and judgemental hater or even republican(jk)! Other possible synonyms that may flood the mind are straight-laced, boring, prude, un-passionate, or reserved. I am here to testify that Christ is none of those things. That's right. I said testify- to tell you from personal experience and biblical truth what I know is real. So, "christians" as they're known today..... I don't like 'em.

I also don't like people. People bug the (insert christian swear word here) out of me! It's like the country song says, "God is great, ROOTbeer is good, and people are crazy..." People ARE CRAZY! And they're not Christ followers. So, I don't like them. IF people lived to represent Christ in all His attractiveness, namely unselfishness and LOVE, then I'd find them more appealing. But they don't, so I don't.

Then, there's God. Because my selfish nature doesn't allow me to, I cannot say He's always pleasurable to my life's palette. His constant focus is for my focus to be outside myself! On Him and others! That doesn't always set well with me. However, that's why some people don't like me either...same reason I don't like them.

So, what am I saying with all this? What's my point anyway? Why the ranting about how I don't like anyone? It's simple.... to reveal a truth. It's a bunch of horse-puckie(excuse my christian french, I inserted it myself this time). I'm here to confess that I don't like people, yes, but guess what? It's my own stinkin' problem!

MY PROBLEM! I need to get over it and change starts with me. And guess what? I'm finding "christians", people, and my dear heavenly father more palatable every day. WHY? Because even though I don't like them, I LOVE them. Becoming unselfish, laying down my "self" and picking up the cause of Christ everyday, makes liking people and God irrelevant. Actually, where God's concerned, it gives me new perspective and I become MADLY IN LOVE with God.

Remember, as a child, when you'd do something naughty that made you completely unlikable and your mom would say, "you know, I really don't like you right now, but I still love you." That's love smothered in grace and mercy; at least when it comes to christians and other people. When it comes to God, that's love smothered in trust and faith. I can begin to find the world to be a more desirable place and so can you. Simply forget about liking people and love them. Whether you like someone or not keeps the focus on you and your happiness. Love is selfless. Love changes EVERYTHING. That's classic cause and effect right there.

Jen's Coaching Questions
1. Ha ha...clearly I was in a mood the day I wrote that! Do you find yourself resonating with this piece though? ...I don't like you. I love you....Why or why not?
2. Did your parents every tell you they love you but they don't like you right now? How did that make you feel?
3. It's said that love covers over a multitude of sins. How so?

Tit for Tat - We're Entitled

Introductory Thoughts: Entitlement. We're all tired of it yet entitlement as a movement keeps growing. Read my thoughts on it today. I would like to add one more thought however... although life is a gift, I DO believe that once we have it, we have the right to keep it...just wanna make sure you always hear my heart.

Read: Luke 17

It is NOT your birthright to get something back, just because you gave something. Nor is it your birthright to expect something, ANYTHING simply because you live. It is absolutely NOT your birthright, to whine about what you don't have because , as it happens, someone else DOES have it. Do you hate me yet? You surely have the right, RIGHT? I just had the audacity to tell you you have NO Rights! In fact, I had no right to do that SO....let me do this for you:

continuing to read this to its entirety ENTITLES the reader to feelings of being offended and allows the extension of judgmental attitudes toward the writer, in which they may thereby respond by giving said writer an "ear-full" .

I certainly have no problem with that. Since, I'm taking the time to write this, I do feel entitled to a little feedback. :)

Let's see....have you heard any of these phrases lately? "I want____, Give me___, Buy me___" How 'bout, "It's not fair! You owe me!"Or here's a list for ya: "I'm a college graduate, so I deserve a high paying job, I'm a senior citizen so I deserve young people's respect, We weren't put on this earth to suffer, so life owes me a break" Right now, you're all shaking your heads in agreement, shouting a cognitive AMEN! However, I bet these following phrases, designed to feed our entitlement tendencies are about to give you an AHA moment. Oh yes, I know your favorites..." Because you're worth it (Loreal), Have it your way (Burger King), Think what we can do for you (Bank of America)."

We hear all of the above constantly but we only like the latter phrases and feel we should never have to hear the previous ones. Although, WE'RE the ones saying them BECAUSE of the latter ones! Why we all feel so entitled, people?! For goodness sake, **if life is a GIFT, why do we EXPECT so much more just because we have it?** We're ALIVE! That IS our gift! Now, let's go use it to give to others before it's taken away. We're certainly not entitled to it...our life that is. It is, after all, a gift.

With feelings of entitlement at epic levels, we've become a people who deserve "the good life", are experts at the blame game should anything go wrong, and increasingly lazy and self-indulgent. We're also failing to be all we can be since, after all, whether we succeed or fail, we're entitled to the benefits of success in excess! (I.e. all kids get a trophy, Americans have debt, etc) we want the prize and to be counted as equals without any effort. Again, I say, why we all feel so entitled, people?!

I think it's this: Disappointment, greed, failure to own one's behavior and even more valid reasons such as; lack of love, respect, boundaries and proper expectations as a child hold a very real possibility to foster **feelings of loss and emptiness that could lead to resentment and anger , ultimately paving the way to entitlement.** To some degree, we all have entitlement feelings. We think we're owed for who we are or what we have. It's a "one way street" mindset that keeps us focused on what we're owed, not what we can do or give to others.

This week I read Luke 17:7-10 in the New Testament and was refreshed by the attitude of the text.

7"Suppose one of you had a servant plowing or looking after the sheep. Would he say to the servant when he comes in from the field, 'Come along now and sit down to eat'? 8Would he not rather say, 'Prepare my supper, get yourself ready and wait on me while I eat and drink; after that you may eat and drink'? 9Would he thank the servant because he did what he was told to do? 10So you also, when you have done everything you were told to do, should say, 'We are unworthy servants; we have only done our duty.'"

What?! Are you not refreshed also? Did the text not do for you what it did for me? Oh! I know why! Duh! I forgot to remind you of another little piece of text. Philippians 2:3," Do nothing out of selfish ambition or vain conceit, but in humility consider others better than yourselves." Whew! There. You forgot for a moment that we're ALL servants, meant to serve each other. You were feeling entitled there for a moment weren't ya? Anthony B. Robinson, a columnist, said this, " Entitlement signals a rejection of the very DNA of America. Our national genetic code, at least at one time, was patterned on respect for the common man and woman. It was sequenced by a belief in the dignity of human life that's not the consequence of having, but of being." I love it. And because, as McDonald's would say, "You DESERVE a break today", I won't hound you anymore, but will leave you to your own conclusions and thoughts as you're certainly entitled to them. God bless!

Jen's Coaching Questions
1. In what areas of your life do you find yourself entitled?
2. How can we protect ourselves from feelings of entitlement?
3. What are your initial thoughts when reading Luke 17:7-10?

Reflections on Joshua 13

Introductory **Thoughts**: I wrote this for Pursuit Church Live pastored by Angela Craig. At Pursuit Church Live, they walk through scripture together. We were currently making our way through Joshua.

Read: Joshua 13

Today we will take a look at chapter 13. This is the first thing I blatantly notice:

"Dude, you're old; incredibly old; so old you don't have much time left...so get to work!"

What if someone said that to you?

Not only that, what if that someone was God? Joshua chapter 13 is basically a review of how two and a half tribes of Israel have already received their inheritance but nine still need their's. This is all keeping in mind that the Levites don't get an inheritance, as their inheritance is the Lord.

However, the emphasis is Moses gave two and a half tribes their inheritance, but it's up to Joshua to divy up the rest for the other nine and he's ridiculously old so he needs to get a move on it!

I don't know about you but my thoughts if God were to tell me to get to work and that I'm old would be:

- Ouch! No rest for the weary, huh? I thought these were supposed to be my "golden years"?
- Ah! I'm running out of time?! Like how much time are we talkin"? Is this a here today gone today kinda scenario?!
- God has work for ME to do. I MUST do it.

Indeed. There's no rest for the weary with God. He is our rest when we obey. If anything, we can look at his words as if they're a compliment! He still thinks Joshua (or we) got what it takes dentures and walkers or not!

Yes, you may be running out of time, but none of us ever knows how much time we have anyway, and that should never be our main focus. We should always just live and work while it's still called today.

And the bottom line? God has given specific tasks to specific people for a specific reason. Joshua should be honored that he was chosen. So should we.

Jen's Coaching Questions

1. What sticks out to you when you read Joshua chapter 13?
2. How would you respond if you were Joshua?
3. How would you feel?
4. What are you being asked to do today that only you can do?
5. What is your timeline to do it?

I Wonder

Introductory Thoughts: I wonder...is basically just another way of saying Jen's mind is unwinding again. This time I find myself wondering why we can be so hypocritical and ungracious, especially when someone much more important than us is probably...smiling.

Read: Matthew 18:3, 19;14; Mark 10:13-16; Hebrews 11:6; Matthew 7:1-9

It occurred to me that often we seasoned Christians criticize, chastise and basically judge the actions of those still young in Christ; and I wonder if Christ looks at the same things we see and instead, smiles... I know. Incredulous, right? Don't get me wrong. I'm not talking about sin. I'm talking about the actions that to us "older" Christians seem immature. The things that make our eyes go wide, followed by a slight roll, or cause us to puff up our chests with a "humph". You know, the things that bring out our index finger in it's best "tisk tisk" fashion.

The incident that made me wander to this wondering was an interaction with my five year old yesterday. He caught wind that if he worked hard at his chores and cleaned his room, a monetary or otherwise material surprise was to be had. He worked so hard even to the point of making his brother's bed and cleaning his brother's room! It was so evident that his main goal was simply to be rewarded in a materialistic way BUT, as his parent, I didn't look down on him in judgement and disgust but I found myself *smiling*.

Many times in life we compare the love of God the father to a worldly father.

Yes, my son is five. And, yes, clearly his motivation was to see what he could get....so completely immature. HOWEVER, my perspective as his parent was quite different. I saw a little boy that after EVERY CHORE, made sure to see that I had been watching or else he would proudly report what he had just accomplished. He did this with eyes beaming and shoulders tall and proud. Yes, all in anticipation of what he could possibly get. BUT, as his parent I also realized this...He knows that I love him and whatever reward I have in store is going to be a good one, EVEN IF HE DOESN'T EXACTLY KNOW WHAT IT WILL BE. And clearly, he was also excited to make me proud... proud enough to want to reward him. So, no. I didn't think, "good grief. He's just doing this for the reward." As his parent who knows he's young and immature yet making progress in the right direction, my heart was warmed and I DID smile. I was touched that he wanted to make me happy and that he trusted and BELIEVED that indeed, I would do what I said and reward him.

And there it is folks, what most see as immaturity may simply be childlike faith and anticipation in what the father has for them. Young christians don't know what's ahead of them and they may be in it for what they're gonna get, BUT it's because they KNOW that whatever they're gonna get comes from a loving and gracious God that has nothing but good things for them! It's the right of a youngin' to love and trust their father with all love and abandon. Then with maturity, will come service with true sacrifice, but in the meantime, at least they're servin'! So, as elders in Christ, let's just smile at that.

I don't know about all this, but I sure do wonder...AND I smile.... because MY son KNOWS I give good things when he does what I ask.

Jen's Coaching Questions
1. How have you been judged by other Christians?
2. How have you judged other Christians?
3. What are some things that those newer to the faith may do that we might roll our eyes at but Jesus would smile at?
4. How can we offer those newer to the faith grace without advocating iffy behavior?

Tie or Tithe

Introductory Thoughts: Oh no....a post on giving. Here we go...

Read: Malachi 3:10; Luke 4:12; Deuteronomy 26

I get passionate about tithing. Why? Many reasons. The one that sounds more judgmental being, "I don't like people stealing from God". The one covered in love being, "I want God's promises fulfilled in your life. The one full of the most risk, the most faith AND the most prone to opportunities for modern day miracles being, " God said to TEST Him in this" (Malachi 3:10).

Let's start with the last reason. We hear all our Christ following lives that God gave us a brain so use it and don't "test Him" (Luke 4:12). This, of course, means we should use wisdom in our everyday lives. Examples would be: if you're sick, use your head and go to the doctor and don't just sit around waiting to be healed; That's what God created the profession of doctor for. Or, as in Jesus' case, don't just go throwing yourself into danger because the bible says " He will command his angels concerning you, to guard you carefully" (Luke 4:11)...That's just trying to manipulate and "test" God and God doesn't play that.

However, in this ONE area, God goes ahead and says to TEST HIM! Most people who don't tithe because they believe it's not wise to spend/give money they don't have are given a **free pass here!** God bless you for wanting to be good stewards of your money but in this case, God says, TEST HIM! I don't know about you, but I'm kind of intrigued by the adventure such an admonition holds. Even the most nervous or skeptical person IF THEY TRULY BELIEVE IN AND TRUST JESUS has got to love the idea of where that may lead! Of course, if you're in the red in your bank account and have a ton of medical bills to pay, it seems scary and unwise. However we also know that God works all things according to our good (Romans 8:28) and God's promises are true (2 Corinthians 1:20)

Some would say, but I SIMPLY HAVE NO MONEY for tithes after paying my mounds of medical bills! To that I say, you just answered your own problem in your statement. You said you have no money "after". Tithes should be the first fruits of your income (Deuteronomy 26). The testing of and faith in God comes when you pay your tithe FIRST and then watch the miracle of how God provides for your medical bills or whatever money woes you may have.

My second reason for being passionate about tithes, "I want God's promises fulfilled in your life" is very similar to my last explanation. He says, "test Him and see if He will not open the flood gates." The Word also says, "without faith it is IMPOSSIBLE to please God, but you must believe He exists and EARNESTLY REWARDS those who SEEK Him"(Hebrews 11:6) He wants to reward you and fulfill His promises. **Don't tie His hands** by not having faith and not seeking Him!

Lastly, please don't rob God. He gives us all we have. He gives us our family, our jobs, our talents and our resources. He is point blank asking for the first ten percent of all our increase. It's HIS anyway because **HE GAVE IT TO US** so don't steal from God and do what YOU think is best with the money. We know how that can end up....Malachi 3:6-10; Proverbs 16:25.

* "A poverty mentality says I can't tithe. A rebellious mentality says I won't tithe. A kingdom mentality says how can I not tithe? He's been so good to me. How can I give more?" - Dustin M. Bates

Jen's Coaching Questions

1. What are your thoughts on tithing?
2. If you've tested God in this way, how has it worked out for you?
3. What do you think about the quote above by Dustin M. Bates?
4. Why do you think the bible usually says to not test God, but in this ONE case, encourages us to?

Colossians 3:17

Introductory Thoughts: Time for a little self check. Use today's shorter devotional as an opportunity to reflect in prayer and do some recalibration where needed.

Read: Colossians 3:17

WHATEVER you DO or SAY, do it as unto the Lord. As you embark on another day, ask yourself before you do or say anything, is this to the glory and service of God?

Am I eating a box of cookies as unto the Lord or unto myself?
Am I disciplining my child....
Am I speaking to my husband....
Am I drinking this alcohol.....
Am I doing these drugs.....
Am I caring for my home....

Am I working at my job....

Am I spending my money....

Am I utilizing social media....

Am I serving in church....

If you're not doing it as unto the Lord or if it's an action that's impossible to do as unto the Lord, maybe you shouldn't be doing it. Now, back to Colossians 3:15 which is two verses previous, let the peace of God RULE in your hearts. :)

Pray for me in all of this, I'll pray for you!

Jen's Coaching Questions

1. Do you think it's possible to eat a whole box of cookies as unto the Lord? Because, honestly, my answer would be some-times yes! Why do you think I'd say that?

2. What are some things that you are doing or not doing for the Lord?

3. Why are we called to do everything as unto the Lord?

4. How can you keep the idea of doing everything as unto the Lord at the forefront of your mind?

Bible Ghost Stories: Who is the Holy Spirit?

Introductory Thoughts: This article I authored was originally written for Fire Bible for kids aged 6-12 and those that teach them.

Read: Isaiah 9:6; Acts 2:38; John 14:16-17; Acts 1:8

It is often difficult for kids and even adults to understand who the Holy Spirit is and how He helps us. Let's see if we can navigate through these questions by asking a few others...

Who's ever done something wrong? Or felt bad about it? Who's been brave when most would be scared or needed help to make right decisions?

If you said yes, you may have had help from Jiminy Cricket (your conscience) or if you said yes AND you've given your life to Jesus, you may have had help from the Holy Spirit!

Who is the Holy Spirit and what does He do? Is He wind? Is He fire? Does He give you super powers? Maybe you've heard some of these explanations/comparisons before. Let's find out who He really is once and for all!

Have you ever heard of the TRINITY? God in *three* persons? What?!?! God in three persons? How is that possible? Well, remember. With God, ALL things are possible! The trinity is God, Jesus, and the Holy Spirit. They are three in one. We know who God is...He MADE us. We know who Jesus is...He SAVED us. But who is the Holy Spirit?

Think of it like this: Think of your Dad or Mom. They are ONE person, but they are PARENT to you, spouse to each other, friend to their friends, employee to their job, and son or daughter to their parents. They're ALL THESE DIFFERENT PEOPLE but still just ONE PERSON! So, it is basically the same with the trinity.

This helps us understand the trinity but we still need to know who the Holy Spirit is. Let's find out what the bible has to say about him!:

1) Who is the Holy Spirit? Isaiah 9:6

2) How do you get the Holy Spirit? Acts 2:38

3) Where does He live? John 14:16-17

4) What does He do in our lives? Acts 1:8; John 14:26; John 16:8; Galatians 5:22-23

Work as detectives and really answer these questions and discuss them with others if possible.

So, if God MADE us, and Jesus SAVED us, then we can conclude from these versus that the Holy Spirit HELPS US stay in fellowship with Him who saved us and remember why and by WHOM we were made! The Holy Spirit HELPS the purposes of Jesus and God which is why they're all three together of ONE MIND and PURPOSE!

Jen's Coaching Questions

1. Who would you say The Holy Spirit is?

2. How would you describe The Holy Spirit?

3. How would you describe the trinity?

4. How does the Holy Spirit help you?

Relationships Take Three: The Concept of Three

Introductory **Thoughts**: Originally posted on http://www.her-voiceblog.us/?p=1515

Read: 2 Timothy 3:16; Ecclesiastes 4:12

When I got married, one gift I received from a dear lady in our church was a beautifully framed poem, titled "Marriage Takes Three". It went like this,

I once thought marriage took
Just two to make a go,

But now I am convinced
It takes the Lord also.
And not one marriage fails
Where Christ is asked to enter,
As lovers come together
With Jesus at the center.
But marriage seldom thrives,
And homes are incomplete,
Till He is welcome there
To help avoid defeat.
In homes where Christ is first
It's obvious to see,
Those unions really work,
For marriage still takes three.
 By: Perry Tanksley

I love this poem; and I think it's so true....not just for marriage, but for all relationships. It holds true for friendships, parent/ child relationships, work relationships...all relationships.

The Rule of Three

Then today, I was reminded of the poem again when scrolling FaceBook as I came across this post of wisdom from a young gal, Ashlee, in our church (you'll see I inserted the word relationship for my own purposes):

"When we put our relationship with Jesus as our number one priority, every other situation/relationship falls under His direction, His strength, and His authority. "

If He is our number one thought, passion, and hope, then His power will direct our lives and relationships. His Grace will abound and His strength will pick us up. "I am the Lord, and there is no other" Isaiah 45:5

Do you see the patterns of three that I do? " HIS direction, HIS strength, HIS authority..." and "... our number one thought, passion, and hope..." If we do as the poem says and put " Jesus at the center", making Him as Ashlee says, "our number one priority", we and our relationships fall under His blessed rules of three (direction, strength, authority) because we give Him our top three best in (thought, passion and hope).

The Three Day Rule

There's another rule of three when it comes to relationships of any kind. The Three Day Rule. This rule provides that you take three days to pray, think and reflect before making any major decisions regarding a relationship and before having any serious discussions that could be sensitive to a relationship. IT IS A LIFE SAVING AND RELATIONSHIP SAVING RULE OF SAVING GRACE! This Three Day Rule gives you time to give God all your thought, passion and hope in any given situation so that you can acquire His directions, strength and authority.

Thinking of breaking up with a boyfriend? Three Day Rule. Thinking of marrying him? Three Day Rule(unless you've been taking more like three months or three years! haha) Have to have a heart to heart with a co worker who's stepping on your toes?

Three Day Rule. Have to dole out some tough love to a friend?
Three Day Rule. TRUST ME.

There's a Latin phrase, "omne trium perfectum" which dictates
that everything that comes in threes is perfect, or, every set of
three is complete. There's also a little God breathed phrase in
Ecclesiastes, useful for teaching, training and correcting, that
pretty well compliments the Latin one, "a strand of three cords
is not easily broken" -(2 Timothy 3:16; Ecclesiastes 4:12). So,
use the Three Day Rule today to consider the Rule of Three because Relationships take three.

Jen's Coaching Questions
1. Why do relationships need three to make them work?
2. What would happen to a relationship of any kind if God was
    not involved?
3. What do you think about The Three Day Rule?
4. Have you used The Three Day Rule?
5. What would you add to The Three Day Rule?

Matthew 18:8

Introductory Thoughts: The proof is in the pudding.

Read: Matthew 18:8

So if your hand or foot causes you to stumble or sin, cut it off and throw it away. It's better to enter eternal life with only one hand or one foot than to be thrown into eternal fire with both of your hands and feet.

So if your money causes you to be greedy or self important, burn it. It's better to enter eternal life as a pauper than to be thrown into eternal fire with your bank account.

So if your facebook account causes you to neglect your family or work, close it. It's better to enter eternal life without 50+ likes

and comments than to be thrown into eternal fire with 500+ followers and friends.

So if your alcohol causes you to occasionally get drunk, get rid
of it. It's better to enter eternal life without the occasional beer
than to be thrown into eternal fire with your excuses of "it started as only a social drink" or "I only do it once in a while to unwind and only SOMETIMES does it ever get out of hand".

So if your anger causes you to upset your children and spouse,
get it under control. It's better to enter eternal life as one who
bites their tongue and holds back their fist than to be thrown
into eternal fire with your "justifications".

So if your sarcasm causes you to hurt people's feelings or mis-
represent Jesus, stop it. It's better to enter eternal life with a
few less laughs from people who think you're so funny than to be
thrown into eternal fire with the pride of your wit.

So if your television causes you to run out of time to read your
bible, turn it off. It's better to enter eternal life knowing more
about Jesus and less about the Kardashians than to be thrown
into eternal fire with the knowledge of who got the rose on the
Bachelor.

So if your _____causes you to STUMBLE OR SIN, cut it
off. It's better to enter eternal life without it than to be thrown
into eternal fire with your _____.

The _____ is different for everyone. What's causing you to stumble and sin today?

Jen's Coaching Questions

1. What is the _____ that is causing you to stumble and sin today?
2. Are you willing to cut out your _____ to save yourself?
3. How would this blog post relate to idols?
4. How would one argue that the _____ in people's lives are their idols?

Ugly Stinky Feet People

Introductory Thoughts: God bless the hard to love people, the extra grace needed people. You know who I'm talking about. What we need to consider, however, is that sometimes others might think that person is us!

Read: I Corinthians 12; Romans 10:15

In the church, we are ONE body. But sometimes our bodies have ugly, stinky feet and it's hard to maintain peace and unity with these members....every time you look at them and anytime you get too close, you simply say, "EW!" and may even shiver! Well, if you're dealing with ugly, stinky feet people, I say show them some LOVE... take them out, spend time with them, treat them to a pedi! ... you'll soon find your investment has made them beautiful in your eyes! Besides, we need the feet! Sometimes there's a good reason they be so ugly and staaankAY; did you ever consider that they might be the ones kicking, walking and running the race while carrying the weight...and it's taken it's toll? Remember, beautiful are the feet of those who bring good news!

Jen's Coaching Questions

1. Think about the Ugly Stinky Feet people that you know. Why do they cause you to scrunch up your nose?
2. How do you give extra care to the parts of the church body that need more care and discretion?
3. I've always thought that people become like who they hang out with? Do you think if some of the beautiful people spent more time with the not so lovely that they might both influence each other as iron sharpens iron? Why?

How to Practically Parent in an Ever Increasingly Broken world

Introductory Thoughts: Whether you have children or not, this post is for you. It's for you because you probably influence children OR their parents. It's for you so you know what others go through.

Read: Phillippians 2:3; John 13:35; John 16:33

Whether or not you have children of your own, we all have kiddos in our lives one way or another. You may be an auntie, teacher, coach, or babysitter; this article is for you too. That being said, every momma (and I don't know because I'm not one, but I'm guessing daddy too) who serves the Lord, has that moment of panic shortly after bringing a brand new tiny life into the world...."What have I done? I am now responsible for this life, for leading their little heart into relationship with Jesus. From here on out, it's heaven or hell for this little one." It's a heavy and sobering thought to come to the realization that someday your precious angel will have to make a decision for themselves about whom they will serve.

Then, add on top of that the current situation of things. We thought when we were growing up it was hard dealing with peer pressure, depression, bullies, hormones etc, but now? Add to that, a world going ever toward a path of degeneration.....more school shootings, legalization of immoral things we never imagined, and more.

No matter where you stand on any of the issues, there's no denying that a vast amount of Christian parents are feeling a level of panic. "How do I protect my babies? How do I parent them? I've got to raise them right AND keep them safe! These things must be overturned! Things must go back to 'normal'." I'm here to tell you that I'm one of them. I'm human, so yes....I initially panicked, but guess what, I know the one who holds the future and His word tells me that when I respond to what's happening around me, I should remember three things:

"Do nothing from selfish ambition or conceit, but in humility count others more significant than yourselves" (Philippians 2:3).

"By this all people will know that you are my disciples, if you have love for one another" (John 13:35).

"In this world you will have trouble, but take heart! I have overcome the world!" (John 16:33).

Let me tell you the facts, Jack. This world is NOT going to change for the better. As we near end times, things will become worse and worse. They have to. We've been told so (see 2 Timothy 3:12-13). So, as Christ honoring parents who are scared for our littles, what should our response be? Panic? No. Practical parenting in an inevitably changing world? Yes.

So, as Christ honoring parents who are scared for our littles, what should our response be? Panic? No. Practical parenting in an inevitably changing world? Yes.

That being said, I fully realize that none of us really knows how to handle these scenarios and these days we're living in. However, as I stated earlier, we know the ONE who does and we KNOW He has ours and our children's best interests at heart. Below are some practical tips and thoughts to keep in mind when navigating today's waters of parenting:

This world will only get crazier and we CAN'T freak out with every new occurrence that leads society further down the drain.

We need to give our kiddos practical tips on safety and lead them to further passion for Jesus.

Be honest with your kids (about what they may encounter in restrooms, in viewing other's relationships and more) in a way they are able to understand.

Help your child to know that some things are a form of brokenness that saddens the heart of Jesus AND as such, should be treated as something broken should be treated....with respect, gentleness, love and the goal of restoration.

Broken things should be treated as if they're broken...
with gentleness and the goal of restoration.

Remember, you catch more flies with honey than vinegar. The reality is these things do make us a level of upset but when discussing them, we should not raise our fists and rant on social media or elsewhere.

Encourage open conversation with your littles. Ask what they think and what they're encountering....regularly. They must see us remain CALM and not shocked at what they share.

We cannot shelter our children from all the ugliness. We can only equip them to deal with it. We should not panic and rant at what the world is coming to. We should only be humble, considering others better than ourselves, constantly displaying the love of Jesus.

I'd like to thank my friend, Heather, for her inspiration behind this article. She also recommends taking in Craig Groschel's podcasts on parenting.

Jen's Coaching Questions

1. How can you give your kids practical safety tips while encouraging them to lean on Jesus?
2. How can you be honest with kids in a way they can understand?
3. How do you feel about the idea that brokenness in the world should be treated as broken things are treated: with respect, gentleness and the goal of restoration?
4. Why must we remain calm and not shocked at what our little ones tell us?
5. Why can't we shelter our children? Why is the only option to equip them?

Everything is Awesome

Introductory Thoughts: Originally posted at www.nwministry.com. I'd also like to share a little side note: I went to school with Chris Pratt! (enter fangirl scream here) I didn't run in his circle of friends but I remember seeing him at school many times and how funny he was. He graduated the year before me.

Read: Phillippians 2:3

If you have kids or anything to do with them, you've probably watched the latest Lego Movie. There's a hit song, however annoying, that tends to "stick" with viewers of the movie. It goes a little something like this:

Everything is awesome. Everything is cool when you're part of a team. Everything is awesome when you're living the dream.

These simple and elementary lyrics serve as a great reminder for leaders in ministry. If you're in ministry, you're probably following your calling, which SHOULD mean that everything is awesome and you're living the dream...but this ideal is not always the case. Ministry can be stressful, people can be hard to work with, and dreams can fade. What do we do about this?

Everything is Awesome

Get an awesome perspective! Need a fresh perspective as a leader? Need a little encouragement and light at the end of the tunnel? Then realize EVERYTHING IS AWESOME!
Dictionary.com defines awesome as:
1. inspiring; an overwhelming feeling of reverence, admiration, or fear; causing or inducing awe: an awesome sight.
2. 2howing or characterized by reverence, admiration, or fear; exhibiting or marked by awe.

By this definition, everything IS awesome! Look around you. Are you not in awe of nature? Of your church or the world around you?

I'm in awe of things around me every day. God, obviously, is AWESOME. My church is awesome. Those are two positive forms of awe that strike me. I'm also in awe of how crazy this world can be and people as well...even in the church sometimes. Whether good or bad, everything is awesome.

Everything is Cool When You're Part of a Team

I attended a worship meeting last night under the leadership of Jammie Bigbey. He reminded us that we are to consider others better than ourselves (Philippians 2:3). We are here to equip people to be better leaders and draw people to Jesus. He reminded us that we are NOT here to be a solo act or super star.

If you're experiencing stress or conflict with fellow ministers or others in your church (or other areas in your life), take inventory. Are you lifting THEM up and EQUIPPING them? Is the vision of your ministry focused on bringing people to Jesus or is it about having the perfect "show" on Sunday? Take time to develop the people God has placed in your life, encouraging them to use their God-given talents to HIS glory. When you do this, you're part of a team and everything is cool.

Living the Dream

Once you have a perspective of everything being awesome and a goal of working on a team to the Glory of God and salvation of souls, then you're living the dream. Billy Graham once said,

"The dual love for God and love for others is like the positive and negative posts on a battery: Unless both connections are made, we have no power."

You're living the dream, when you're loving God and people. Your ministry will be powerful! Now that's awesome!

If you haven't heard the song, google it. Then, when leadership gets rough, just remember, EVERYTHING IS AWESOME!

Jen's Coaching Questions:
1. How have you found yourself needing fresh perspective as a ministry leader or just an every day Christian?
2. Are you surrounded by a good team of people? How do you all serve each other?
3. How are you living the dream and helping others to live the dream?

Relationships STILL Take Three - Never Trust Your Friends

Introductory Thoughts: I lost one of my best friends in life, in part I believe, because I was making her an idol and God was gracious enough to save me from myself. This blog was born of that.

Read: Mark 12:30; Matthew 10:37, Exodus 20:3

Never trust your friends?! What on earth does that mean? Okay, it may be a little extreme but it means don't put all your eggs in one basket. Don't put all your eggs in one basket unless...that one basket is God. Don't put all your eggs or **trust** in one basket that is not God.

According to goodenglish.org, it's a piece of advice that means you shouldn't concentrate all your efforts in one area as you could lose everything. When considering relationships, I would amend the definition to "you shouldn't place all your trust in humans, because they're fallible (they're not God) and you can come out big on the losing end". Humans **will** misunderstand you. Humans **will** occasionally be selfish and abuse you.

The bible says in (Mark 12:30) that "you shall love the LORD your God with all your heart, with all your soul, with all your mind, and with all your strength.' This is the first command-ment." All your trust should lie in Him. In every relationship that we have with other people, our relationship with God must always be our top priority. Jesus says in (Matthew 10:37) "He who loves father or mother more than Me is not worthy of Me. And he who loves son or daughter more than Me is not worthy of Me. We are also told in (Exodus 20:3) not to "have any other gods/idols before Him".

When we trust our friends before or instead of God, we make idols of them. When our friendships become more important than waiting on and spending time with God, we make idols of them. When we care more about what our friends think of us, than what God thinks of us, we make idols of them. When we work to please our friends with our life choices rather than God, we make idols of them....and we are no longer **worthy** of God.

Not only that, but when we make friendships that important, we tend to *believe* we can trust them with anything, that they would **never** hurt us, and inevitably, we **are** crushed and left reeling. It does not mean that your friends are bad people and not to be trusted. It means that your friends are human (just as you are) and although can be trusted with many things, they can also be trusted to eventually let you down whether intentionally or unintentionally because they're simply **not** God.

Are friends or your spouses letting you down? Do you feel you can't trust anybody? Is your heart too fragile lately? Then repent. Tell God you're sorry; and if needed, tell your friends or your spouse you're sorry.

Then, remember every situation that we come into, especially if it's with other people, we should come into in Jesus' name because He says (Matthew 18:20) "where two or more are gathered in my name, there I am with them". Relationships only fall apart when one person (or both) loses sight of Jesus and becomes selfish, looking for their needs to be met in the other person. **Only** Jesus can be the true source of our peace, love and joy..

When you make God the middle of everything, you can never be too let down to the point you find yourself reeling, because you know where your source of peace, love and joy come from. Your **stability** is in the **one** you can **always** trust.

Remember back to part ONE of this two part article, Relationships Take Three. Make God the center of all your relationships today. Let Him love you unconditionally and be the source of all your trust and hope so that your relationships glorify Him. This protects you **and** your friends. This keeps you in line with His commandments. Trust me. :)

Jen's Coaching Questions

1. How have you idolized friendships in the past?
2. Why is it easy to idolize friendships or people?
3. How do you think it would feel to be on the receiving end of idolization?
4. Describe a time God has graciously saved you from idolizing.

If you Love Me, Keep My Commands

Introductory Thoughts: If you don't obey Jesus, does it mean that you hate him?

Read: John 14:15; Hebrews 4:12; Romans 7:15-24

In LifeGroup through my church last week, we were asked to read John 14:15 and then to imagine Dr. Phil asking as he would, "how's that goin' for you?"

John 14:15 reads:

If you love me, keep my commands.

Cue Dr. Phil's "how's that goin for you?" ... and my group's immediate reaction was OUCH.

Obviously, thinking of the verse that way made us feel like we're missing the mark because we're not constantly carrying out Jesus' commands and therefore we must not love Him. It hurt. It cut us right through to the core. I looked around at the fallen faces of the ladies in my group and I knew there was more to this. I smiled, looked at the girls and reminded them,

- The bible is a double edged sword, a book of checks and balances, of tension and release (Heb 4:12). Reading a verse like this is to help us judge the thoughts and attitudes of our heart. Therefore,
- Remember even Paul said in Romans 7:15-24 that although He wants to do what Jesus commands, he often fails. Is it because he doesn't love Him? NO. It's because he is not yet perfect and he can't be perfect until he is made like Jesus. Until then, he has to pick up his cross daily (Luke 9:23). Therefore,
- The verse John 14:15, is meant to create healthy tension.

We can't let something like John 14:15 condemn us, but we must let it convict us. Are we keeping His commands? Not always, but it doesn't mean we don't love Him. It means we need to be aware of our need to keep persevering (Heb. 112:1-2) and have faith that He is the author and finisher of our faith....and that that kind of faith is true love, a love that drives us, compels us to keep His commands.

Jen's Coaching Questions

1. What is the difference between conviction and condemnation?

2. If you read John 14:15 and then were asked "how's that going for you?" what would your reaction be?

3. How can we look at John 14:15 as conviction rather than condemnation?

4. Why might someone consider obedience their love language to God?

All Leaders Eventually Make a Wrong Decision

Introductory Thoughts: I do realize I've addressed leadership twice in this book, but the fact is, we are ALL leaders in some capacity. You may be a coach, a parent, an influential peer or something else. But we all lead in some capacity.

Read: Genesis 16; Joshua 9; 2 Samuel 11

All leaders eventually make a wrong decision. All leaders are human. Humans make mistakes. Therefore, all leaders eventually make a wrong decision. This is even true for good, Godly leaders like in the bible.

Why do leaders make wrong decisions? Yes, they're human. We covered that. But what are those human characteristics that direct us to wrong decisions? I believe there are several answers but that the most common is probably trying to make things happen our way in our timing: Manipulation.

For example, consider Abraham and his actions that brought Ismael into the world. Abraham was good and Godly; he believed and cherished the promise God made him that we would be the father of a nation. However, he couldn't wait and fully trust God's timing and methods so he took it upon himself to help/manipulate the situation with Hagar. But guess what? God doesn't need our help. (Genesis 16)

Or think about Joshua when he foolishly made a pact with the Gibeonites. The Gibeonites deceived him saying they were far away when they actually lived very close. Instead of consulting God first, Joshua just believed them....another grave mistake by an otherwise great leader! (Joshua 9:23)

Lastly, what about David and Bathsheba? He would have her NO MATTER the cost! (2 Samuel 11)

ONLY GOD'S METHODS CAN BRING SUCCESS. We need to wait on the Lord in all circumstances. We need to wait on Him to:
-Fulfill His promises in HIS way
-Give us direction in big decisions
-Give us the desires of our heart

However, if we fail, we are NOT failures. We are not without hope.

Even though we make bad decisions, it doesn't mean that we have "fallen too far from grace" or that God is not fulfilling His promise, or you didn't hear right from God, or that we are bad leaders. It simply means that we had a "human" moment where our faith wavered, even if without our realizing it, and we thought God needed "our help" to bring our dreams to pass. If anything, take it as a "humbling moment" to remind yourself where your faith lies....but whatever you do, DON'T lose heart! Otherwise, you'll really fail. Simply repent and move on trusting God to take things one step at a time in His way. (Psalm 51)

Jen's Coaching Questions
1. What kind of bad decisions have you made as a leader?
2. Why did you make those bad decisions?
3. Why do ONLY God's methods bring success?
4. How have you "lost heart" due to a wrong decision you made?

Share Your Struggle

Introductory Thoughts: When we share our weaknesses, we strengthen others.

Read: Hebrews 11:1; Psalms

Sunday, I prayed with a gal at church who with pain in her eyes confessed that she's terribly depressed because no matter how much she prays or reads her bible she "feels nothing". Now, this gal in particular I know a little bit, and happen to know she's very vivacious and full of light so for her to admit this is quite a devastation for her.

As soon as she shared with me, my mind went back in time about 20 years when my grandpa, a well known and well loved pastor turned evangelist turned pastor; a man who was full of life and light, told me about his drought. He said he went through a period of over a YEAR when he felt absolutely NOTHING from the Lord. God was distant. He felt defeated. I was shocked! How could someone like grandpa ever feel distant from God?! However, grandpa KNEW with His head what his heart was currently struggling with...God was the real deal and that He DID indeed love him. So, he continued....

Grandpa continued to pray. Grandpa continued to read his bible even though God felt so very far away. He said it was a very hard time but he remained faithful to a God he knew was faithful despite how he might be feeling. In the end, when the feelings of intimacy returned, it was better than ever!

I shared this with my gal friend at church and then we prayed. She was immediately encouraged....and I was only able to encourage her in that way because my famous hero of a grandpa in my eyes was vulnerable with the truth.
Be vulnerable with your truth today while STILL glorifying the truth of God...and share your struggle. It could really save someone.

Jen's Coaching Questions
1. How have you been vulnerable with your truth lately?
2. What would others be shocked to know you struggle with?
3. How have you experienced spiritual drought before?
4. What methods help you to be sure of what you hope for and certain of what you cannot see?
5. How can you hold yourself accountable to being vulnerable?

Practically Spiritual and Spiritually Practical

Introductory Thoughts: I LOVE when someone else's story inspires me. My friend Mandy, has inspired me in more ways than one, but here is her latest.

Read: John 2; John 6, Romans 12

I've been thinking a lot about the practical side of ministry and the spiritual side of ministry. I'm 38 years old and have been raised in the pentecostal faith. The first half of my life it seemed as though faith, religion and ministry were more spiritually focused. The second half of my life I've felt, and focused myself, more on the practical side. What I want to address here is balance.

We know balance is healthy. Anytime we tip the scales in any area of life, the excess (the heavy side) becomes a heavy burden; and when we start dragging something heavy, our efforts slow down.

How did this play out in my opinion when the scales were tipped toward the spiritual? First and foremost, as my friend, Evan Westerfield puts it, we created a majority of people who were chasing an experience(spiritual) without solid biblical literacy(practical).

Why is this an unhealthy balance? Because spirituality comes from God and when you don't have God as your source (from filling your heart and mind with His word) then, spirituality starts coming from yourself. Once things originate from self versus God, we have a very unhealthy state that can not only harm our own spiritual experience but those of others....and GASP!... those of new to faith converts!

How does this harm happen? People operate in "spiritual gifts" without actual Holy Spirit power creating confusion and fear. People create their own idols of themselves and their "gifts". When God is not the originator of something as well as the result (being glorified), we have a HUGE imbalance that leads to big trouble... AND can be difficult to tip back in the right direction.

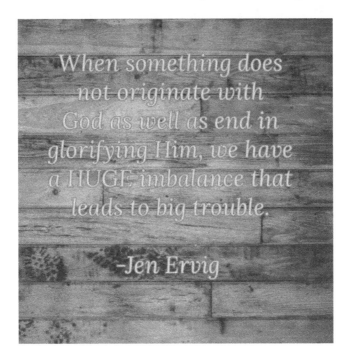

Now, let's look at the last 16-ish years and tip the scales toward practicality. Why did believers make the shift? Well, probably because the actual Holy Spirit opened our eyes and showed us we had a situation to remedy! People were over-spiritualizing many aspects of Christian living and it was needlessly turning people off from what should be a very attractive aspect of our faith. The Holy Spirit is attractive. We've ruined the Holy Spirit's reputation and needed to save face. We owed it to the Holy Spirit to apologize and remedy the damage to His image we created.

But as people tend to do, we tipped the scales too far. We started shirking the spiritual for fear of offending or seeming weird. The result was effort that made sense but seemed to be lacking something....a certain "spark" if you will.

How do we fix it and put the scales in balance? Well, let me tell you a story from this week...

I met with my friend, Mandy Downey, who started a women's LifeGroup of just three ladies this last January. The group exploded to about 13 in a matter of weeks! These women are faithful to attending every week, are inviting their friends....doing life together and are on fire for God like I've never seen! I mean they literally do life together! They babysit each other's kids, meet for fun outside of LifeGroup and carry each other's burdens all of their own volition (Mandy doesn't orchestrate it).... and most of them just met two months ago! How does this happen? How is Mandy's LifeGroup Ministry such a success and making Jesus famous? So, I asked her, "Mandy, how is your group so successful? What would you tell a fellow LifeGroup leader who wants to know your secret?"

She said, (in my best paraphrase)... "What kind of experience are you creating for the people when they walk in? There's the practicality of being a welcoming hostess; fluffing the pillows, putting out freshly washed blankets to snuggle into the corner of the couch in, setting out all the tea options and the coffee... but there's the spiritual too. I set aside time every week and pray for each of my ladies as I walk through the living room, and I'm old school so I anoint the room with oil also."

Perfect balance. Do you realize that when her ladies walk in Mandy's door every week, without even realizing why, they probably feel deeply loved and an incredible peace? Simply because Mandy practically prepared AND invited the Holy Spirit into the home to join them. Every week when those ladies come, the Holy Spirit is already there to welcome them because Mandy invited Him but she didn't make a an obnoxious show of Him. How could they want to be anywhere else?!

Now, I'm not asking you to drench your leather sofa in EVOO (insert Rachel Ray's voice) and make a slip n slide of your living room set. I am suggesting that we go back to the creator of balance, spirituality, and practicality and let Him lead. Listen for that still small voice and watch as the scales come back into balance.

Read more on practical/spiritual balance that brings about miracles much like the miracle of Mandy's LifeGroup:

God uses a boy's practical gesture and adds the Holy Spirit - John 6:1-15

God uses the practicality of filling barrels with water and adds the Holy Spirit - John 2:1-11

Romans 12:2

2 Timothy 3:16

James 2:20

Jen's Coaching Questions

1. In your opinion what does it look like to be practical and spiritual?
2. How have you experienced the same tipping of the scales that I have?
3. What do you think it means to overspiritualize?
4. Why is being too practical with no spiritual aspects a bad thing?

Let God Move In

Introductory Thoughts: I feel like I've come through a rough season of loss lately, but beautiful things come out of some really ugly stuff. You can take that to the bank!

Read: Psalm 34:18; Hebrews 13:5; Genesis 50:20

Loss and distance. It's hard and lonely; especially if you had no intention of losing something or someone; especially if you were working towards closing the gap on distance. However, that's how loss and distance usually works isn't it? We don't initiate it or mean to anyway, and yet there it is.

A family member dies

A friend pulls away

Someone you love moves

A colleague makes it clear they have no intention of befriending you

Loss and distance. It leaves an empty space that we search to fill with something as soon as we can. Self pity, cynicism, hopeless-ness, sadness. I used to fill the voids I didn't ask for with some of these things. These options are easy and quick fillers when we just need the gap to close and the "empty" to go away. The only downside is the empty comes back and bigger than before.
I found a better way.

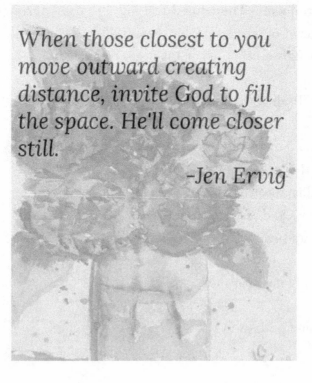

When those closest to you move outward creating distance, invite God to fill the space. He'll come closer still.

-Jen Ervig

Invite God to fill the space. He always longs to come closer still. In fact, I'm not completely convinced that some losses occur and distances are created to make room for me to invite God to come closer still. For me, when God moved in...

Death taught grace like I'd never known

I found I was worshiping friendship and making it an idol and can now refocus

I ministered to my friend and learned to cherish people while I have them

I shrugged off the slight...because it's not about me.

I became thankful for loss and distance because God brought me something out of all of it. He's close to the broken-hearted, will never leave you or forsake you, and never wastes a hurt. (Psalm 34:18; Hebrews 13:5; Genesis 50:20)

You need never feel empty and lonely for long, friend!

Jen's Coaching Questions
1. How have you experienced loss and distance?
2. What's the difference between something lost and something that's just distant?
3. How have you seen God come closer still in times of loss and distance?

Keepin' Cool in the Fire

Introductory Thoughts: Trust God and Chill.

Read: Daniel 3

Hives. I have hives; a skin rash triggered by an irritant. In my case, the irritant is a lotion I shouldn't have used. My face, neck, arms and legs are now on fire and covered in tiny little bumps and it's all I can do to keep from scratching til I bleed. This need to scratch is driving me crazy and stressing me out big time. I'm cranky because I want to scratch and my skin is crawling and burning. And I'm cranky because I have a million things to do and can't focus on most of them. It's even hard to write this blog except for the fact that the typing keeps my fingers from scratching!

Stressing does not help hives. Oh no. It makes them worse. I feel like I have a cactus stuck to my face but I must keep cool in the fire.

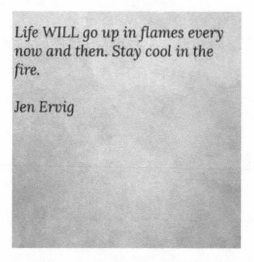

Life WILL go up in flames every now and then. Stay cool in the fire.

Jen Ervig

Isn't that how it goes when anything in life goes up in flames due to an "irritant"? We have to find a way to keep our cool. We have to find Jesus in the furnace just like Shadrach, Meshach and Abednego (Daniel 3). No matter what the irritant is that put you or your situation ablaze, it's now imperative that you do three things:

1) GET RID OF THE IRRITANT. If you know what started the fire, nix it now. I won't be using that lotion ever again. Now, Rach, Shach and Benny couldn't help that ol' Neb threw them in the fiery furnace, but a lot of times we can help what starts the fire. Maybe your fire started by a comment, bad habit, people you shouldn't associate with, etc... If you can help it, nix it.

2) KEEP YOUR COOL. Easier said than done, right? But pray, keep busy while you're in the fire and think/meditate on good things. Let God worry about the flames. He'll take care of them. Trust God and chill.

3) DON'T ADD FUEL TO THE FIRE. Scratching my hives doesn't help. Stressing doesn't help. Whatever you may be doing to add fuel doesn't help. If you find yourself adding fuel, refer back to number 2.

Okay, guys. I'm done typing now. Pray for me while I go rub myself in hydrocortizone and take more benedryl. This cactus will fall off eventually.

Jen's Coaching Questions
1. How can one realistically "trust God and chill?"
2. What do you think was going through Rach, Shach and Benny's minds while they were in their fire?
3. Why does stress and worry add fuel to the fire even if we didn't start the fire?
4. How would it feel to testify about coming through the flames unharmed?

What to do When You Stink at Praying

Introductory Thoughts: Okay guys, I STINK at praying. Honestly. I never know what to say so I just call on the Lord a lot and ask that He be given glory in whatever the situation is. I'm always jealous of those who seem so eloquent in how they speak to our King. Thank God that we don't have to be conversational experts.

Read: Psalms 34:15; Daniel 9:18; I John 5:14; James 5:16

What to do when you stink at praying? You pray. Plain and simple. Honestly, if you stink at praying, or feel you do, it's probably all in your head...for the most part. I mean, I suppose it's true that some people stink at conversation. Prayer is conversation and conversation takes skill. Well, good conversation takes skill...and if you're reading this, it's because you wish to be good at your conversational skills with the love of your life, Jesus! However, truly, good conversation (especially with Jesus) is just taking the focus off yourself and placing it on the other person. No need for eloquent speech or thoughts. But, if practical tips are what you're looking for, let's see what we can do...

Good conversation (especially with Jesus) is just taking the focus off yourself and placing it on the other person. No need for eloquent speech or thoughts

So, I searched up, as my 10 year old would say (searched up haha), "how to be skilled at conversation" and this popped up:

Talk slowly. Typically, good talkers don't rush into a conversation. Hold more eye contact. Most people keep eye contact about 2/3 of the time or less when they talk.

Notice the details.

Give unique compliments.

Express your emotions.

Offer interesting insights.

Use the best words.

Okay, so let's see how we can translate this to our conversational skills with Jesus:

Talk slow. I don't think this one matters so much. God can listen to you at any speed. If you got something to say, go ahead and spew it out.

Hold more eye contact. Tough to do when we can't tangibly see God. I think for prayer, this could mean having a posture of staying focused on the one you're speaking with or praying to. Don't let yourself be distracted by every "squirrel" that runs by. Have you ever heard the admonition to "be where you're at"? Show respect for God by being attentive to Him and your time with Him...don't be half hearted in your prayer time.

Notice the details. When you're conversing with a person this means to notice their tone of voice or body language. When you're conversing with God, it means to notice those things when reading His word or to be sensitive to The Holy Spirit while you're praying. When you notice the details, the other person sees that you genuinely care about what's taking place between you.

Give unique compliments. Woo the one whom you love and praise with praise that He'd only hear from you in the way that you convey it.

Express your emotions. We connect through emotion. It's one of the benefits that emotions provide!

Offer interesting insights. God knows what you're thinking but He wants to hear you express it. Indulge Him.

Use the best words. When talking with people, this means to improve our vocabulary. I believe for prayer, it means to memorize scripture and pray the scriptures. The bible is the best written piece of work in existence. Use it!

So, what to do when you stink at praying? Just pray...and never stop! Sure...use the skills above and cultivate them...but honestly prayer is the best form of conversation because all you really have to do is open your heart and God will do the rest.

Jen's Coaching Questions
1. Why do we sometimes feel like we stink at praying?
2. What is it like when you feel "in the zone" with your prayer life?
3. How would you explain your conversations with God to someone who has never prayed?

God - The Perfect Party Planner

Introductory Thoughts: This book is for me one of the best gifts I've ever received from God my father at the best party He's planned for me yet.....AND...the surprises keep coming!

Read: Hebrews 11:1

It can be so disheartening to work, desire, seek, and anticipate something only to have it never seem to come to fruition. And worse than that,...to feel or even be told that indeed it won't! I've experienced a lot of heartache in recent months and some by well meaning people. I have a dream to speak, yet was told I'd never have a platform. I wish to be a pastor (which has a shocking story in and of itself) but I'm not educated or mature enough. I want to write a book, but I don't have that kind of talent and will never find an audience.

Yet I keep stepping forward. I don't even know why! The only explanation I have for my continued effort is my favorite verse, Hebrews 11:1. Then, things started to happen for me out of the blue:

- Opportunities at education
- Platforms for speaking and writing
- Promotions at work

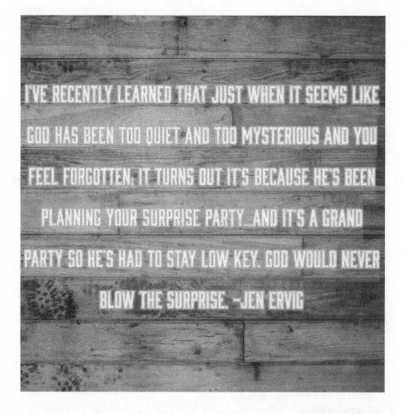

I kept wondering why things weren't happening for me. Why God wasn't stepping in and making a way....ah, but He was!

He just wanted the absolute BEST bang for his buck and He KNOWS I fancy a good surprise! Thank you, Lord, for all you've done for me! This is the best party ever!

Jen's Coaching Questions
1. How have you felt forgotten by God?
2. What was the actual outcome of those feelings?
3. What is the best surprise party you've ever been given?
4. What is your favorite verse?
5. How do you integrate your favorite verse into your life?

Closing Thoughts as This State of My Mind Winds Up!

Thanks for journeying with me this month through what's made my mind unwind or wind up as it pertains to this life we live. I'd love to hear what gets your heart and noggin' going and how you invite Jesus into that process. Feel free to message me at jensmindunwinds@tumblr.com. I also want to thank several people for believing in me in all I set out to pursue:

- My husband, Randy Ervig
- My parents: Ken and Marilynn Snodgrass
- Two of my favorites: Lisa Smith and Nicole Keel
- My bosses: Andrew Munoz and Nik Baumgart

- My cheerleaders: Jodi Detrick, Tammy Emineth, Angela Craig and Velvet Steel
- Those who heard my humble plea to review my book: Emily Hutchinson, Kerri Pomerolli, Jodi Detrick, Mark Gungor, Tara Beth Leach and The Harts.
- Lastly, and most importantly: My Jesus

What follows are my initial thoughts for when I do write about my process of grieving my brother...

The above is a poem and painting I did for my mom

The Day My Brother Died
Finally Understanding the Love of God Through a Nightmare

The day my brother died? Well, that's problem number one. We don't even know. Was it the 8th of May? Later? He was found on May 13th. A possible five days or so of being alone, above ground, doing what expired bodies do when left unattended. Too real for you? I'm sorry. It was and is most very real.

"Your brother is dead." My mom told me on my cell phone as I was pulling up to my boys' school to drop them off...kindergarten and 3rd grade. My brother was a hero in their eyes. In fact, my oldest was wearing a leather Marine's bracelet he had just made two days before. He couldn't wait for my brother, the Marine, to see it. I hadn't yet realized that now he'll never see it.

"Your brother is dead." It's like I can't comprehend it. Was it suicide? He did have PTSD, depression and anxiety...but no, he would never...and the autopsy confirmed it. Was it murder? He had received threats from people....Overdose from alcohol? But he was sober, wasn't he? (yep...another autopsy confirmation). How do we know he's not just on a trip somewhere???

How?! Why?! When?! These questions, questions I DEMANDED answers to would go unanswered. Unanswered even now 16 months later as I finally sit down to write about it.

After dropping the boys off, I continue driving to work at the church where I'm a pastor's assistant. I'm in shock as to be expected....my mom still on the phone. "How? How do you know?" I ask my mom. I can't remember what she answered but I remember saying," I can't wrap my head around this right now. I have to go".

Somehow I received the story. My dad went to work where my brother also worked in another area. My brother's boss asked my dad if he'd seen my brother and my dad started to.....wonder. You know the kind of wondering when a sort of alarm goes off inside of you because recent things that haven't made sense start to make sense but the only kind of sense that can ONLY lead to nothing good? Yeah...it was that kind of wonder.

You see today was Tuesday. The Tuesday after Mother's Day. The Tuesday after the Saturday we were supposed to have lunch with my brother and his new girlfriend, but it didn't happen because he never answered the phone or our texts to see what the plan was. The Tuesday after Mother's Day! My brother was a mama's boy and never called his mom to wish her a happy day. She wrote it off as he had just started the graveyard shift due to a promotion and his sleep was all messed up....but he didn't call Monday either. Then Tuesday... nobody knows where he is.

My dad leaves work and goes straight to his apartment. No one is answering. He goes to the office and says he needs to see his son, can someone please let him in. Legalities permit them from doing so but they go up and do a "well check" on their resident. Within minutes they come down...."I'm sorry, sir. It looks like your son has passed."

Has passed. Has passed so far that he's not even recognizable anymore. They refuse to let my dad see him in that state. Has passed. Only fingerprints can now even prove that it's him. He's passed.

For me, this is problem number 2. I want proof. Fingerprints won't cut it. I want to see him. I need to see his face, that his eyes are closed and that the rise and fall of his chest is indeed absent. He's only 30 after all. Passed?

Passed from what? From life to death? That's stupid! He's 30! 30! And you couldn't really call what he had "life" unless he was with his family. PTSD and depression made "life" not so full of life. And where did he pass to?.....problem number 3.

It was problem number 3 that would have me in torment for months to come. However, it was problem number three that would lead me into a deeper understanding of the love of God that no matter what, can never fully be realized this side of heaven.

Jen's FaceBook blurb proclaims, "Strong independent black woman who don't need no man. Actually, Norwegian and I need Mike and Ike(s)." Nothing could be more true.

Currently working as the Connections Pastor at The Grove Church in Marysville, Wa, Jen strives to bring people closer to Jesus while encouraging them to not take themselves too seriously. She's worked as a ghost blogger for an SEO company for many years and has been a credentialed minister for 7 years. She also recently acquired her Assemblies of God Coaching Credential. Her writing has appeared in Angela Craig's book, "Under One Umbrella", as well as Reflections for Pursuit Church Live and HerVoice Blog at NWMN.

Jen has been married for 15 years and has two boys, aged 13 and 10. She considers her family her favorite Missions Team to work with and her favorite Missions field? Disneyland. Hey, someone's gotta be a ray of the hope of Jesus in that 90 minute line.

CPSIA information can be obtained
at www.ICGtesting.com
Printed in the USA
FSHW01n1946300818
51920FS